NFL TEAM STORIES

The Story of the
SAN FRANCISCO 49ERS

By Jim Gigliotti

Kaleidoscope
Minneapolis, MN

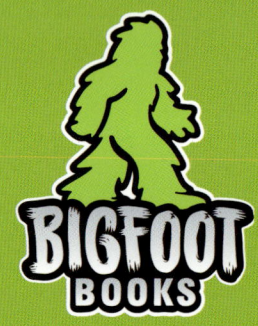

The Quest for Discovery Never Ends

....

This edition first published in 2021 by Kaleidoscope Publishing, Inc.

No part of this publication may be reproduced in whole or in part without written permission of the publisher.

For information regarding permission, write to
Kaleidoscope Publishing, Inc.
6012 Blue Circle Drive
Minnetonka, MN 55343

Library of Congress Control Number
2020936092

ISBN
978-1-64519-245-9 (library bound)
978-1-64519-313-5 (ebook)

Text copyright © 2021 by Kaleidoscope Publishing, Inc. All-Star Sports, Bigfoot Books, and associated logos are trademarks and/or registered trademarks of Kaleidoscope Publishing, Inc.

Printed in the United States of America.

FIND ME IF YOU CAN!

Bigfoot lurks within one of the images in this book. It's up to you to find him!

TABLE OF CONTENTS

Kickoff!... 4

Chapter 1: 49ers History.. 6

Chapter 2: 49ers All-Time Greats 16

Chapter 3: 49ers Superstars 22

Beyond the Book.. 28
Research Ninja.. 29
Further Resources.. 30
Glossary 31
Index 32
Photo Credits 32
About the Author.. 32

KICKOFF!

Jimmy G.

The 49ers quarterback has always been a star in San Francisco. Some of the greatest passers of all time have played for the Niners. Y.A. Tittle led the team in the 1950s. Joe Montana took the club to new heights in the 1980s. Steve Young was a star in the 1990s. All three are in the Hall of Fame. These days, the 49ers have another great QB. He's Jimmy Garoppolo. You can call him Jimmy G! Can he be the next to lead the Niners to glory? Let's meet the team and find out!

Jimmy Garoppolo

Chapter 1
49ers History

The 49ers began playing in 1946. They were part of the All-America Football Conference. That was a **rival** pro league to the NFL. The Niners were one of the AAFC's best teams. In 1950, the NFL invited the 49ers to join their league. It took a while for San Francisco to become good. Then the team made up for lost time!

WHAT'S A 49ER?

Gold was discovered in California in the mid-1800s. People from all over the world rushed to settle there. They wanted to make their fortune. The team was named after those settlers. Many of them arrived in California in—1849!

Joe "The Jet" Perry runs for the 49ers in this 1955 game.

John Brodie led the Niners in the 1960s.

In 1970, the 49ers won their first title. They were champions of the NFC West. They won the West the next two years, as well. Each time, they could not get past the Dallas Cowboys in the playoffs. That soon changed. The 49ers hired Bill Walsh as head coach in 1979. The team **drafted** quarterback Joe Montana the same year.

The pieces fell into place. The 49ers won the NFC West in 1981. This time they beat the Cowboys in the playoffs. They needed an incredible play called "The Catch" to do it. Check out pages 14-15! After beating Dallas, the 49ers went on to win their first Super Bowl!

FUN FACT

Walsh and Montana perfected a short passing attack called the "West Coast Offense."

Joe Montana

The 49ers were the best team in the NFL in the 1980s. They won the Super Bowl four times. Three came with Bill Walsh as coach. Then Walsh **retired**. The team kept right on going. George Seifert became coach in 1989. The 49ers won the Super Bowl again that year!

Nothing could stop them. Steve Young took over for Joe Montana as quarterback in the 1990s. The 49ers were champs again in 1994. They were the first team to win the Super Bowl five times!

Steve Young

Jim Harbaugh

The 49ers had some good players in the early 2000s. But the team fell on hard times. In 2011, the 49ers hired Jim Harbaugh as coach. He was a former NFL quarterback.

Harbaugh was a fiery leader. He inspired his players to be better. He made the 49ers winners again. The team made the playoffs three years in a row. The 49ers made it to the Super Bowl in the 2012 season. They lost a very close game to the Baltimore Ravens. Fans were disappointed, but they knew the 49ers were back!

Kyle Shanahan became the head coach in 2017. He is the son of Mike Shanahan. Mike was an assistant coach for the Niners in the 1990s.

The 49ers started slowly under Kyle. The team stuck with him. It paid off in 2019. The 49ers won 13 regular-season games. It was their most in eight seasons. They won the division. They went on to the Super Bowl. The future looks bright again for this team with a proud history!

FUN FACT
The NFC Championship trophy shown here is named for famous coach George Halas.

TIMELINE OF THE SAN FRANCISCO 49ERS

1946

1946:
The 49ers play their first game.

1970

1970:
The team wins its division for the first time.

1981

1981:
Super Bowl champs!

1984

1984:
The 49ers win 15 regular-season games. They win the Super Bowl again.

1994

1994:
The 49ers become the first team to win five Super Bowls.

2012

2012:
The Niners lose Super Bowl XLVII to the Ravens.

2019

2019:
San Francisco wins the NFC championship.

THE CATCH

Just mention "The Catch" to any 49ers fan. Even longtime NFL fans can tell you about it. They all know exactly what you mean!

The famous play called "The Catch" came in the 1981 playoffs. The Niners trailed the Cowboys late in the NFC Championship Game. Joe Montana rolled to his right. Dallas defenders closed in. They nearly got him!

Montana leaned back and lobbed a pass into the end zone. Dwight Clark leaped as high as he could. He caught the ball with his fingertips. Touchdown! The 49ers beat the rival Cowboys.

Two weeks later, the 49ers won their first Super Bowl. The Catch was a great play. It helped the 49ers become a championship team in the 1980s.

Chapter 2
49ers All-Time Greats

We have already met several great 49ers quarterbacks. Frankie Albert was another of the team's all-star QBs. He made the **Pro Bowl** in the team's first year in the NFL. John Brodie was another all-star. He played 17 seasons for the team starting in 1957. Beginning in 2000, Jeff Garcia made three Pro Bowls in a row.

Two 49ers QBs have won the Super Bowl MVP Award. Joe Montana did it three times! Steve Young did it once.

Joe Montana

FUN FACT

Steve Young was the second lefthanded QB to win a Super Bowl. The first was the Raiders' Ken Stabler.

Jerry Rice

Every great passer needs somebody to catch the ball. For Montana and Young, that was Jerry Rice. He was one of the best receivers ever. He was a first-round draft choice in 1985. He played 16 seasons for the team. He went on to catch more passes that anyone else in NFL history. He had more receiving yards and touchdowns, too.

The team's fans called Rice the "G.O.A.T." It stands for "Greatest of All Time." The fans have a good case. The point of football is to score touchdowns. In NFL history, no one scored more TDs than this Niners receiver!

Rice was carried off the field by his teammates after his final game.

The 49ers have had some great runners, too. Joe "The Jet" Perry was a star in the team's early days. Roger Craig was fast enough to run around defenders. He was strong enough to run through them! Frank Gore became the team's all-time leading rusher in the 2000s.

Defensive back Ronnie Lott was one of the 49ers' best players on defense. He was a star for the Super Bowl teams of the 1980s. Linebacker Patrick Willis made seven Pro Bowls in a row starting in 2007.

Ronnie Lott

49ERS RECORDS

These players piled up the best stats in 49ers history. The numbers are career records through the 2019 season.

Total TDs: Jerry Rice, 187

TD Passes: Joe Montana, 244

Passing Yards: Joe Montana, 35,124

Rushing Yards: Frank Gore, 11,073

Receptions: Jerry Rice, 1,281

Points: Jerry Rice, 1,130

Sacks: Bryant Young, 89.5

Chapter 3
49ers Superstars

Jimmy Garoppolo helped the 49ers make the Super Bowl in 2019. "Jimmy G" doesn't always throw the most perfect spiral. His statistics are not the best in the league. Joe Montana didn't always throw perfectly, either. Other QBs had better numbers than Montana, too. But Jimmy G is a winner just like Montana. Jimmy G ended the 2019 regular season with 24 career starts for the 49ers. The team won 19 of those games!

Why do footballs fly farther with a spiral? The spin helps the football cut through the air more quickly and fly straighter.

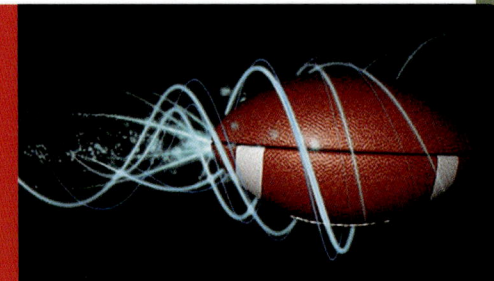

Jimmy G's favorite target is George Kittle. He is one of the best tight ends in football. Kittle set a record for his position with 1,377 receiving yards in 2018. He made his second Pro Bowl in 2019.

George Kittle

FUN FACT
Fullback is a type of running back who focuses on blocking.

Kittle is a strong blocker, too. So is fullback Kyle Juszczyk (say "JOO-zik"). They help give the 49ers a great rushing attack. Big tackle Joe Staley also opens up holes with his blocking. He played his thirteenth season for the team in 2019. He has been an all-star six times.

Richard Sherman

Richard Sherman is one of pro football's great cornerbacks. In 2019, Sherman made the Pro Bowl for the fifth time in his **career**. Fred Warner is a top young linebacker. He led the 49ers in tackles in 2019.

Defensive end Nick Bosa comes from a football family. His dad and older brother were first-round NFL draft choices. The 49ers drafted Bosa in Round 1 in '19. He had a big impact as a rookie. He posted nine sacks. He made the Pro Bowl.

The Niners lost the Super Bowl in 2019. They want to return again and win it. With talent like theirs, it won't be long!

FUN FACT
Nick Bosa was the NFL Defensive Rookie of the Year in 2019.

Nick Bosa

BEYOND
THE BOOK

After reading the book, it's time to think about what you learned. Try the following exercises to jumpstart your ideas.

RESEARCH

FIND OUT MORE. Where would you go to find out more about your favorite NFL teams and players? Check out NFL.com, of course. Each team also has its own website. What other sports information sites can you find? See if you can find other cool facts about your favorite team.

CREATE

GET ARTISTIC. Each NFL team has a logo. The 49ers logo shows a big SF in an oval. Get some art materials and try designing your own 49ers logo. Or create a new team and make a logo for it. What colors would you choose? How would you draw the mascot?

DISCOVER

GO DEEP! This book talks about Jerry Rice as the "GOAT," the greatest of all time in the NFL. Check out other players who have been called a GOAT. What about in other sports? Are there GOATs in baseball, basketball, golf, or tennis?

GROW

GET OUT AND PLAY! You don't need to be in the NFL to enjoy football. You just need a football and some friends. Play touch or tag football. Or you can hang cloth flags from your belt; grab the belt and make the "tackle." See who has the best arm to be quarterback. Who is the best receiver? Who can run the fastest? Time to play football!

RESEARCH NINJA

Visit www.ninjaresearcher.com/2459 to learn how to take your research skills and book report writing to the next level!

RESEARCH

DIGITAL LITERACY TOOLS

SEARCH LIKE A PRO
Learn about how to use search engines to find useful websites.

FACT OR FAKE?
Discover how you can tell a trusted website from an untrustworthy resource.

TEXT DETECTIVE
Explore how to zero in on the information you need most.

SHOW YOUR WORK
Research responsibly—learn how to cite sources.

WRITE

GET TO THE POINT
Learn how to express your main ideas.

PLAN OF ATTACK
Learn prewriting exercises and create an outline.

DOWNLOADABLE REPORT FORMS

Further Resources

BOOKS

Levit, Joe. *Football's G.O.A.T.* Minneapolis, Minn.: Lerner Publishing Group, 2020.

Martirano, Ron. *Football: Great Records, Weird Happenings, Odd Facts, Amazing Moments & Other Cool Stuff.* Watertown, Mass.: Imagine Publishing, 2015.

Whiting, Jim. *The Story of the San Francisco 49ers (NFL Today).* Mankato, Minn.: Creative Paperbacks, 2019.

WEBSITES

FACTSURFER

Factsurfer.com gives you a safe, fun way to find more information.

1. Go to www.factsurfer.com.
2. Enter "San Francisco 49ers" into the search box and click 🔍
3. Select your book cover to see a list of related websites.

Glossary

career: the full span of a player's time in a league. Rice had a 21-year NFL career.

drafted: chosen in the NFL's annual selection of college players. San Francisco drafted star Nick Bosa in the first round in 2019.

lobbed: threw in a high, arcing path. Montana lobbed the ball to get it over Dallas defenders.

Pro Bowl: the NFL's annual all-star game. Joe Montana was so good, he made it to eight Pro Bowls.

retired: stopped playing a sport or doing a job. Walsh retired after leading the Niners for 10 seasons.

rival: a fierce and close opponent. The Niners biggest rival is probably the Los Angeles Rams from just down the coast.

rookie: a player in his first pro season. Nick Bosa was the Niners' top rookie in 2019.

sacks: tackles of a QB made behind the line of scrimmage. Arik Armstead led the Niners with 10 sacks in 2019.

spiral: the rotation of a football as it spins without wobbling. Throwing a perfect spiral helps the football go straighter.

starts: games that a player began on the field for his team. Garoppolo made 10 starts and came off the bench in six other games.

Index

Albert, Frankie, 16
All-America Football Conference, 6
Baltimore Ravens, 11
Bosa, Nick, 26, 27
Brodie, John, 7, 16
"Catch, The," 8, 14, 15
Clark, Dwight, 15
Craig, Roger, 20
Dallas Cowboys, 8, 15
Garcia, Jimmy, 16
Garoppolo, Jimmy, 4, 22
Gore, Frank, 20
Harbaugh, Jim, 11
Juszczyk, Kyle, 25
Kittle, George, 24, 25
Lott, Ronnie, 20
Montana, Joe, 4, 8, 9, 10, 15, 16, 19, 22
Perry, Joe, 7, 20
Rice, Jerry, 19
Seifert, George, 10
Shanahan, Kyle, 12
Sherman, Richard, 26
Super Bowl, 8, 10, 11, 12, 15, 20, 22, 27
Tittle, Y.A., 4
Walsh, Bill, 8, 10
Warner, Fred, 26
Willis, Patrick, 20
Young, Steve, 4, 10, 16, 19

PHOTO CREDITS

The images in this book are reproduced through the courtesy of: AP Images: Ray Howard 7 top; Al Messerschmidt 7 bottom, 8, 16; Peter Read Miller 14; Paul Sakuma 15; Al Golub 18. Focus on Football: 4, 16, 20, 22, 24, 26, 27. Newscom: Terry Schmitt/UPI 10, 18; Jon Soohoo/UPI 11; Kiyoshi Mi/Icon SW 12; Kevin Dietsch/UPI 25. **Cover photo:** Focus on Football.

About the Author

Jim Gigliotti was an editor at NFL Publishing for many years. Now he writes books for young readers.